The Life of

St. Francis of Assisi

Written by a child

CASA EDITRICE FRANCESCANA - ASSISI

© Casa Editrice Francescana
Piazza S. Francesco, 1
06081 Assisi (PG)

Prima Edizione Marzo 2009

Text: Rev. Lorenzo Tucci, OFM Conv.
Illustration: Vincenzo Schiantella
English translation: Rev. Thomas Reist, OFM Conv.

Printing: Umbriagraf Terni

Table of contents

Birth

The birth of Francis was a lot like the birth of Jesus. No one really knows the exact year in which Jesus was born, and the same is true for the birth of Francis. Most people think he was born in 1181 or 1182. Everybody knows that Jesus was born in the wintertime when it was very cold. It seems to be the same for Francis. When

Jesus was in the manger, the ox and the donkey breathed on him and kept him warm. Francis, too, probably felt the warmth of sheep, lambs, goats, horses and pigs.
Thus, when Francis grew up and became a friar, the animals were still his friends, especially little lambs.

Little Francis

Peter and Pica were the proud parents of their son, Francis.
Peter was one of the richest men in Assisi. He was a businessman who sold material to make clothing. Some say that his mother, Pica, belonged to a family that came from France. She was known for being very kind and gentle to everyone.
As a child, his parents used to call him "Little Francis". They loved him so much! Little Francis got bigger day by day. Even as a tod-

dler, it was clear that he was a good boy, and smart as well. He liked to play outdoors in the fresh air. He enjoyed taking deep breaths of air and smelling the flowers growing in the yard and the wild flowers in the fields. In the daytime he would chase butterflies. In the evening he used to run after fireflies and listen to the crickets chirp and the frogs croak.

The Dreamer

When Francis was still a young boy, he had a dream about being a knight in shining armor. One day he gave it a try. He made a sword from the branch of a tree. He used the lid of a pot from his mother's kitchen as his shield. The bark from a cork tree became his armor. For a helmet, he carved a pumpkin and put it on his head. Dressed up as a knight, Little Francis paraded around the yard. When his mother looked out the window and saw him, she called

out: "Little Francis, what in the world are you doing dressed up like that?". The child replied: "Mommy, I'm one of the followers of King Arthur, a brave knight of the Round Table!". He ran back and forth waving his sword and shouted: "Crusaders, let us go forward! Get out of here, Saracens! Let us win back the Holy Sepulcher of Our Lord, Jesus Christ!".

The Rascal

Just like children all over the world, Francis was a little rascal. Here are three of his many pranks.

Once, Francis tried to catch a baby sparrow that left its nest for the first time. He climbed up on the roof and followed the bird as it hopped from tile to tile. Francis crawled out to the very edge of the roof. It was truly a miracle that he did not fall and come crashing down.

Another time, Francis played a joke on his parents. He rubbed a very hot pepper against the apples on the dining room table. When his father bit into one of the apples, he began to scream: "Water, water, my throat is on fire!". To stop his throat from burning, Francis' father had to drink the whole glass of water in one gulp.

One afternoon, Little Francis tied a tin can to the tail of his cat. The poor little thing was scared and jittery. It ran out of the house and went through the back streets of town. It made such a ruckus that everyone who heard it came to see what it was. The other children thought it was loads of fun. The grown-ups complained that it was the noisiest and most annoying cat in the world.

The Ring-leader

Francis stood out from all the other children in Assisi. Truly, he had a heart of gold. Francis shared what he had with others and looked out for those who needed help. He always seemed to be happy and smiling. He knew how to bring everybody together for parties and games, and he was happy to pay for the food and drink. Francis also had a good singing voice either for solos or together with his

friends. He even knew how to play the flute and dance. In school, Francis was at the top of his class. He loved to play the part of the comedian and tell jokes. To everyone he would say: "Smile and be happy; don't be sad".

Because he was so fond of having fun and being generous with others, Francis was called the "ring-leader of the neighborhood". It made him happy when his friends would call him their leader.

Peter and Pica, the parents of Francis, were very proud of their son. They thanked God that He gave them a son who was such a precious gift.

The Knight

As the years went by Francis grew up and became a fine young man, full of life and energy. He was good-looking, polite, and well behaved. Francis had a good head on his shoulders and an even better heart. When the young ladies of Assisi pictured the perfect husband, they thought of Francis.

Peter, Francis' father, had plenty of ideas for his son's future. His first wish was that Francis would take over his business and be-

come a rich cloth merchant. He also saw his son as a captain in the army or as a famous knight, like Sir Lancelot. Francis had always dreamt of becoming a knight. Thus, Peter gave him the best set of armor and the finest horse that money could buy. He even bought him the right to be called a knight. Francis was jumping for joy and very happy. It looked as if his dream was finally coming true.

The Calling

Now on the path to knighthood, Francis wanted to join an army. There was a French prince, Walter of Brienne by name, who was enlisting soldiers to fight in the Crusades. The Crusades were "holy wars" between Christians and Muslims. The Muslims had taken over the Holy Land where Jesus lived and was buried. The reason for the Crusades was to win back the Holy Land so that Christians would be free to visit there. Francis enlisted in Prince Walter's army.

Francis said good-bye to his parents, friends, and relatives. He met some other knights who were also joining Prince Walter's army. His great adventure had begun!

Spoleto, a town not far south of Assisi, was the first overnight stop on Francis' journey to join Prince Walter. While everyone else was sleeping, Francis had a vision. Jesus appeared to him and said: "Francis, why are you following a servant instead of his master? Leave these other soldiers and knights behind, and come to serve Me!". Francis knew it was God who was calling him. He quit the army and returned to Assisi.

Everyone thought Francis was a traitor. His friends called him a coward. His father was even ashamed to admit that Francis was his son.

The Crucifix

Francis was a changed man, totally different from what he used to be. From now on, he spent most of his time alone and in silence. He would often roam around in the countryside smelling the flowers and watching the birds in the sky. People thought he was crazy! Children threw stones at him. Often he would go off and visit the

country chapel called St. Damian. This little chapel was not far from Assisi. No one took care of this chapel, and it was falling apart. On one of the walls on the inside of the chapel, there was an old crucifix. One time while Francis was praying, the eyes of Jesus on the crucifix opened very wide. Then His mouth opened, and Jesus said to him: "Francis, go and repair my church. You see it is falling apart!". Naturally, Francis thought that Jesus was talking about the church of St. Damian. Immediately, he started to repair it. He gave it a very good cleaning.

Followers

Francis wanted to give himself totally to God and God alone! That is why he turned away from everything in the world. He began by donating everything that he had to the poor. Then he moved out of his father's house and gave back to his father all the expensive clothes he bought him. For clothing, he started wearing something that looked like a burlap bag. Instead of a belt, he put a rough rope around his waist. He took off his shoes and put on sandals. Francis became a preacher and traveled around proclaiming the Gospel. In

fact, he was a very good example of someone who lived the Gospel. Many of the young people in Assisi admired him and wanted to live the same way Francis was living. Some of them became his followers.

Bernard was his very first follower. Then came Peter, Giles, Leo, Masseo, Rufino, and Angelo. There were many others as well!

They used to pray together as a group. For meals they had very simple food, and not very much of it. They got by with very little. With everyone they met they shared the joyful message of the Gospel. They were the poorest people in town. Thus, people started calling them, "friars minor". Friars meant they were brothers to one another. A minor is someone who lives a very simple style of life, simpler and poorer than other people.

Sister Clare

In Assisi there was a young lady named Clare. She was a member of a wealthy family belonging to the upper class or nobility.

Clare, too, was drawn to the way Francis was living the Gospel, and she wanted to become one of his followers. But, there was one big problem. Clare was a young woman, and there was no way in the world that her parents were going to let her go.

One night Clare could not sleep. She got up and went to Our Lady

of the Angels, the church of the Portiuncula, where Francis and his followers were staying. Clare told Francis all about her call to live the Gospel. Francis was not sure what to do. Should he let her become one of his followers? Or should he send her back to her family? So, he and the friars prayed for guidance to make the right choice, to do what was holy in God's eyes. This was how Clare was accepted into the group in the name of the Lord.

Clare was the first woman to become a follower of Francis. More women followed, and they formed the group known as the Poor Ladies of St. Damian. Later, they were called Poor Clares, the name they go by today.

Lepers

When Francis was a youth, before he responded to God's call, he was deathly afraid of lepers. The minute he saw a leper, he became terrified and would run the other way.

But once he was living with his brothers and was filled with God's grace, lepers became his best friends. He loved them more than he

loved any other people. Francis went out often to be with the lepers. Out of genuine concern for them and moved by God's love, he washed their sores, looked after them, and comforted them.

For their part, the lepers realized they were being treated well, and they rejoiced and thanked God for it.

The other Friars also used to like to spend time with the lepers. They took turns caring for them. Some people found it very difficult – even disgusting – to take care of lepers. Not these friars! Although they were mere mortals, they were more like angels.

The Rule

To help itself stay together, a group usually has a book containing all the rules it agrees to live by. Friar Francis wrote the rulebook for the Friars, and they called it their Rule. This rule was based entirely on the Gospel. Like the rules of all religious groups, it needed to be approved by the Church. So, Francis and his companions went to Rome to get the approval of Pope Innocent III. The pope

read it and thought that it was too strict. He did not think the friars would be able to obey all of its regulations. Thus, he decided not to approve it. But then, with a flash of light from heaven, he changed his mind, and he did approve it. Francis thanked him from the bottom of his heart. Filled with joy Francis and his Friars returned to Assisi, singing the whole way home!

His Brothers and Sisters

When Friar Francis spoke to men and women he called them his brothers and sisters. He even called the animals his brothers and sisters. In fact, he called absolutely everything either his brother or his sister. Here are the things he called brother: the sun, wind, fire, trees, fields, flowers and rocks. And these were his sisters: the stars, moon, earth, water, grass, and leaves.

With this idea in mind, Francis wrote a wonderful poem called, "The Canticle of the Creatures". In it, he even calls death his sister. St. Francis was always praising and thanking God because He created all these beautiful and precious things for the love of His people.

Preaching

One day St. Francis said to Brother Leo: "Come with me, and let's preach to the people of Assisi!". The two friars went on their way. They walked from one end of town to the other with their hands folded, their heads bowed down, and without saying a single word. Afterwards, they returned to the little church of St. Damian, where

they had started out. Brother Leo said to Francis: "Father, we forgot to preach to the people!". The Saint responded: "Brother Leo, we did preach by our silence and good behavior. What we did moved the hearts of the people, and it was pleasing to Almighty God".

Money

The only thing in the entire world that Francis hated was money. He would never call it his brother. In fact, he used to call it "Devil's dung".

One day as Francis and one of his followers were going to preach the Gospel, they came upon a moneybag lying in the middle of the road. It was filled with coins. The young friar said: "Father Francis, let's pick it up, and we can use the money to help the poor!". Friar

Francis did not like the idea. When the young friar kept insisting, Francis finally agreed. The young friar opened the bag, and immediately he threw the bag as far away as he could, because the bag was filled with snakes! Then, Friar Francis warned the young friar and said: "My brother, remember that, for us, money is nothing but a nest of snakes".

The Wolf

One day, Friar Francis went to a town called Gubbio where there lived a very ferocious wolf. It was a mean and nasty beast that frightened all the people who lived in the town. It gobbled up their pets and animals. It even ate their children! Francis, totally unafraid, went right up to the wolf. He petted it, and then he spoke to the wolf, saying: "Brother wolf, I want you to be at peace!". Then,

he gave the wolf a word of advice: "I beg you, be kind to all these people and stop causing them harm". What a miraculous change! From that moment on, the wolf was as gentle as a lamb. It followed Francis around wherever he went. And with children, it was as playful as a puppy!

Preaching to the Birds

One time, Friar Francis went into the forest to pray. There were so many birds that they seemed to cover the trees. Francis started to preach to them, saying: "Brother birds, when you chirp, let it be a song of praise to God. And when you fly high in the sky, may you give glory to God in the highest. Give thanks to the Lord for the food and water that He gives you everyday!".

While Francis preached, the birds sat perched in the trees like perfectly behaved school children seated at their desks. Not a single bird made any noise, and they listened to every single word St. Francis had to say.

When the sermon was over, all the birds – big and small alike – took to flight at the same time. They formed one large flock that looked like a giant cloud in the sky. As they moved and turned in the sky, their wings reflected the rays of the sun, sometimes appearing as silver, other times as gold.

The Dove

One summer afternoon, Friar Francis met a young lad carrying a birdcage containing four baby doves. The boy had snatched the birds from their nest, and he was on his way to the marketplace to sell them. The saintly man said to the boy: "My brother, please let these birds go free. They are supposed to give praise to the Creator. Doves are signs of peace, and they need to carry greetings of peace

to people in the cities and in the countryside". The boy was convinced by the good and holy advice of Friar Francis. He let the birds out of the cage, and they flew away free. Later, this same young lad wanted to become a follower of the holy friar. This he did, and was known as Brother Giles of Assisi.

The Flock

Once when Friar Francis was near Perugia, a city not far from Assisi, he came across a shepherd who was tending his flock. After the holy friar had said hello to the shepherd, he started talking to the sheep and lambs, and to the goats and kids that were in the flock. The animals came right up to him. They raised their heads and fixed their gaze at him, as if they wanted him to speak to them. St.

Francis invited them to praise God. Lo and behold, another miracle! They all began to baa raising their voices together up to heaven to the praise and glory of their Creator.

The shepherd was so amazed at what he saw that he wept tears of joy.

The Baby Hare

One day Brother Juniper found a baby hare in the forest. He carried it back home to the friary. When Friar Francis saw the little animal, he petted it and whispered: "My baby brother, little hare, come up here to me!". The little critter hopped into his hands. St.

Francis drew the animal close to his chest, hugged it, and gave it a kiss. Afterwards, he told Brother Juniper to take it back to its family in the forest. Surely they would be worried and waiting for it to come home, probably afraid that it might be lost.

The Cicada

One day Friar Francis was sitting and praying under a tree. Up in the tree above him, there was a cicada gently chirping.
The holy friar was amazed at the small insect because, with the sound it was making, it was praising its Creator. So, Francis spotted the insect on one of the branches and asked it: "Sister cicada, would you like to come down here with me, and together we will

praise the Lord?". The insect flew right into his hands. They formed a duo, the two of them, Francis and the cicada. Together they sang the praises of God. After a while, St. Francis headed back to the friary. The cicada followed him and sang to him all the way home.

Brother Crow

Once Friar Francis spotted a crow perched atop on old house that was falling apart. The holy man said to the bird: "Brother crow, what are you doing up there all alone?". The crow was barely able to caw, but managed to explain to him that he was badly hurt and not doing well at all. Friar Francis responded: "Come along with me, and the friars will care for you". The poor animal, crippled and sore, hobbled down and found a spot to rest on the friar's shoulder.

The friars welcomed Brother crow into the friary with a big feast. After they had fed the bird, they bandaged up its sores and wounds. They gave it a bed, so it could rest and get better.

This crow stayed with the friars for a long time. It joined the friars, as best it could, in whatever they were doing. When brother crow heard that St. Francis died, it was very sad and unhappy. In fact, the crow was in such grief, it died a short time later.

Bandits

One evening three bandits knocked on the friary door and asked for food and drink, and a bed for the night. The friar who answered the door was mean to them, and he sent them away. Later that evening, Friar Francis heard about what had happened. He scolded the friar for being so unkind. He ordered him to go find the bandits and bring them back to the friary.

The friar obeyed Friar Francis. He went into the forest to track the bandits down. Once he had found them, he led them back to the

friary. The three bandits ate and drank until they were filled. Then they went to bed and had a good night's sleep. In the morning, the bandits were very sorry for all the bad things they had done over the years. They asked Friar Francis and the other friars to forgive them. Then they made up for all the evil they had done by prayers and acts of penance. They stayed with the friars, and later they asked to become friars themselves.

The First Christmas Crib

Many years later, in 1223, Friar Francis thought about celebrating Christmas and wanted to make it as real as he could. He had a great idea. He thought of a living manger scene! The big event took place in a small town called Greccio. Friar Francis set up the manger, and he found a real ox and donkey – just like it was in Bethlehem. A man and a woman from town played the parts of St.

Joseph and the Blessed Virgin Mary. The only part in the whole scene that was not real was the Baby Jesus, who was made of clay. According to custom, at midnight the birth of the Redeemer was announced when the Gospel was read. Friar Francis noticed that the clay Baby Jesus had turned real and even started to move! He opened his eyes and had a sweet smile on his face.

The crib at Greccio was the first of its kind. Friar Francis had found a way to make people see just how real Jesus was when He was born in Bethlehem. St. Francis had invented the Christmas crib.

The Sultan of Egypt

Friar Francis lived at the time when the Crusades were being fought to free the Holy Land from the hands of the Muslims. Thousands of soldiers from both sides were being killed in these so-called "holy wars". These victims were considered to be martyrs. Friar Francis was a peaceful man. Yet, he also had a strong desire to be a martyr. A martyr is someone who dies out of love for Jesus and belief in Him. Friar Francis joined the fifth Crusade that had been called by the pope. He was hoping to die for the faith and become a martyr.

Friar Francis went to Egypt where this Crusade was being fought, and he asked to speak to Malech el Kamel, the Sultan, the leader of the Muslims. His wish was granted, and Friar Francis and the Sultan had a friendly and peaceful meeting. Since the Sultan was so impressed with the simplicity of Friar Francis and his love of the Lord Jesus, he decided to give him a present. He gave him a beautiful ivory horn as a sign of their friendship. When Friar Francis showed this special gift to the Muslims, he was a welcomed guest and was able to travel wherever he wanted to go.

Friar Francis only stayed in Egypt a short period of time. Because his health was beginning to fail, he was forced to return to Italy. After all his fasting and acts of penance, Friar Francis was in a lot of pain. Besides, he was getting up in age.

A Blessing for Brother Leo

Just like Jesus, Friar Francis also had twelve disciples. With these twelve friars he shared his whole life: days and nights, joys and sorrows, good and bad times, health and sickness. But more than any of the others, Friar Francis liked Brother Leo the best. Brother Leo was also a priest who used to hear his confession. Because Leo was such a good brother and he loved him so much, Friar Francis

gave him a special blessing that he wrote down for him on a little piece of paper.

Here are the words he wrote.

Brother Leo, may the Lord bless you, and keep you.
May He show His face to you, and have mercy on you.
May He turn His face to you, and give you His peace.
May the Lord bless you!

The Wounds of Jesus

In 1224, two years before his death, Friar Francis wanted to return to Mount Alverna to pray. This mountain is near the city of Arezzo to the north of Assisi. He used to go there often. This time Brother Leo, who was called "God's lamb", went with him.

It was on this very mountain that Friar Francis received the wounds of Christ, the sacred stigmata, in his own body. While he

was deeply absorbed in prayer, an angel appeared to him. The wings of this angel had the shape of a cross. Rays of light burned holes in the hands, feet and side of Friar Francis, the little poor man of God. Because he had the wounds of Jesus in his flesh, Friar Francis was called another Jesus Christ crucified.

The Stretcher

Friar Francis was no longer able to walk long distances because his feet were pierced and bleeding. But people from the cities and towns around Assisi still asked that he come to them. They wanted to see and hear him, so he could comfort and bless them.

The friars made a stretcher that they used to carry the saintly friar to and from the towns that he was asked to visit. Whether seat-

ed or lying flat on his back on the stretcher, Friar Francis went into the midst of the crowds comforting and blessing everyone. Wherever they carried him, this friar who looked like he had been nailed to a cross, filled the people's hearts with great peace, joy, and love. He truly was another Jesus Christ come back to earth!

Sister Death

By the time Friar Francis was 44 years old, he was very tired. Over the years he had suffered various illnesses, and most recently the sacred stigmata took a toll on his weak body. Also, Francis' community had grown very large, very quickly, and as the leader Francis carried a heavy burden. While he had many fond memories, there had also been troubles and misunderstandings. Francis had suffered a great deal.

Friar Francis sensed that his death was approaching. He asked to be taken to Our Lady of the Angels, to the church of the Portiuncula. This was his favorite place on earth, and it was here that he wanted his earthly life to end. In accord with his wishes, the friars placed his naked body on the bare ground. A stone served as a pillow to support his head, and in his hands he held a book of the Gospels. Sister Death paid her visit in the evening hours of October 3, 1226. As he passed from this world, a mysterious light illumined the night. Skylarks, the saintly friar's little sisters, circled the sky above singing a sad song. But, suddenly, the melody was transformed into a song of great gladness and immense joy.

The Glory of Heaven

Two years after his death, Pope Gregory IX proclaimed Francis of Assisi a saint. Within days, the pope laid the cornerstone of the church where St. Francis' holy remains would be placed. Friar Elias supervised the construction project. The plan for the basilica included two churches, one directly on top of the other. The altar of the lower church is directly over the tomb of St. Francis. The upper church celebrates Francis of Assisi, the Saint in heaven.

The paintings on the walls of the upper and lower basilicas tell the

story of the life of St. Francis and the miracles that happened through his intercession. Cimabue, Giotto, Simone Martini, Pietro Lorenzetti and others, are the artists who created these paintings. They were the best artists of their day. Popes, emperors, kings, princes, and leaders from all around the world have visited this magnificent basilica and have prayed for peace at the tomb of St. Francis. St. Francis was named the Patron Saint of Italy by Pope Pius XII in 1939. Each year on October 4, the Feast of St. Francis, one of the twenty regions of Italy presents the oil that burns in the lamps at the tomb of St. Francis throughout the year. St. Francis is recognized throughout the world as a great saint who helps promote peace in the world and respect for all of God's creation.